Training God's Spies
Developing the imagination in theological formation

Anne L. Tomlinson

Contact Pastoral Monographs

Number 11

2001

ISBN 0 9522485 8 1

Typeset and printed by Q3 Print Project Management Ltd
First published 2001 by Contact Pastoral Trust
New College, Mound Place, Edinburgh EH1 2LX

Introduction

While training candidates for lay and ordained ministry in the Scottish Episcopal Church's Theological Institute a worrying trend became evident to the author. The three-year course which these students pursue comprises modules and projects in the fields of biblical, doctrinal, spiritual, liturgical and pastoral theology, lengthy parish placements, numerous written assignments, weekly seminars and several residential events each year – and all this on top of employment and domestic commitments. Very soon after starting the course, a culture of expediency sets in. Time constraints become the dominating factor, the "need to know" takes over from the "desire to learn more about", and reading becomes directed solely towards the production of the next assignment rather than being a glorious trawl through the uncharted waters of different theological approaches. Lecturers who impart their wisdom in ten-point packages and offer concise distillations of their subject are warmly applauded. Neatness and closure are everything, when the next essay looms so inexorably.

Personal tutors are ever at pains to ensure that the requirements of the course do not overly disrupt home life or put unnecessary strains upon relationships, renegotiating essay deadlines in order to reduce pressure whenever necessary. Attempts however to persuade candidates to build in more *leisure* to their schedules – more time for sport, cinema or concert-going, the enjoyment of novels or poetry, more time simply to "stand and stare" – fall on deaf ears. "There'll be time for that once I've finished the course" is the usual response.

Not only do students eschew leisure activities, but they tend to be suspicious of material listed in bibliographies which is not, in their eyes, overtly theological. The request that they should prepare for a Pastoral Theology module by reading any of the novels of Margaret Forster was greeted with scepticism. With so little time to get through the standard heavyweight works on the subject, why be diverted by such "ephemera"?

As they proceed through the course students become increasingly tired and drained. Ceasing to be fed by music, film and literature, their imaginations become dessicated. Sermons which once had been sparked by scenes from films become more intellectual and cerebral, pastoral encounters more ponderous and laboured, prayer more full of Edwin Muir's "fleshless word". In short, there is a deskilling of intuition.

Four years into working as part of a team responsible for the delivery of the TISEC curriculum, inchoate feelings of dissatisfaction with this dumbing down of creativity began to stir within me. Thus it was that when I chanced upon the following sentence by Sallie McFague, it struck me forcibly:

> If we take the lessons of poetic metaphor seriously, theological training ought to include as a major component the development of the imagination.
>
> (McFague 1975, 105)

Could study of the imagination offer some resolution to my feelings of dissatisfaction as a theological educator? A cursory sweep through the journals of the profession suggest it might. Rebecca Chopp, writing in 1990, suggests the need for new patterns of training in both seminary and academy:

> My argument requires a reinvigoration of the imagination in theological education, and especially the encouragement of aesthetical forms and images that can fund our work and culture ... Today when we face the crises of values, knowledge and power, what is required, at least in part, is a new aesthetic funding, a way of knowing that will be productive of new forms of human flourishing. This will include images and discourses of community, new visions of what it is to be human, new terms for relationships, history, freedom, God, new notions of desire and knowledge. Education, for the future, must emphasise the ability to envision, to produce the aesthetic images and metaphors that fund knowledge, values, community.
>
> (Chopp, 1990, 121)

John Drane and John Reader have issued similar clarion calls (Drane 1995, 5; Reader 1996, 20), but prior to 1998 little had been written about how this might come about in practice. The following was thus offered as a contribution to that enquiry.

The Ministerial Persona

The nature of ministry

> The church is in great danger when the office becomes something
> you sit in rather than something you say.
>
> (Leech 1989, 128)

In these trenchant words Kenneth Leech draws attention to a malaise
currently infecting Anglican theological education on both sides of the
Atlantic, namely the "professionalisation of ministry". His contrasting
of the priest as a person who is daily formed and renewed by contact
with the Church Universal in her praying of the Offices with that of the
priest as "bureaucratic manager" (MacIntyre 1987, 28) is a caricature –
but like all such, it contains a worrying kernel of truth.

The task of theological schools has ever been to prepare students for
the activities of ministry. Since the 1950s however, such activities have
increasingly been viewed "as tasks of an institutionally defined profession" (Farley 1982, 19). Thus in 1967 Owen Thomas could begin a
seminal article in America's most renowned journal of theological
education with "the assumption that the ordained Christian ministry
is properly called a profession" (Thomas 1967, 556), while in the
following year James Glasse's book on the aims of seminary training
proudly sported the title *Profession: Ministry* (Glasse 1968). Two
decades later such a view was to be even more prevalent; it was by
then:

> a generally unquestioned assumption among most mainline Prot-
> estants that the ordained ministry is a profession, and that the
> seminary is a professional school.
>
> (Westerhoff 1982, 153)

The concept of "profession" has a fascinating history. Whilst in the
medieval period it referred to the making of public declaration
(*professio*) to live a life of obedient service to God, by the close of the
Middle Ages understanding had shifted from confession of faith to
possession of particular knowledge and techniques in the fields of
divinity, law and medicine. In modern industrialised societies the
concept is to be understood largely in socio-economic terms, denoting
membership of a trade organised according to function and perform-
ance, and characterised by the following five traits: the acquisition of
a specific body of theoretical knowledge and the development of
particular skills during a lengthy period of education and training; the

testing and accreditation of these prior to qualification and renumeration; relationship to, and service through, a specific social institution and emotional neutrality and adherence to accepted standards of competence and ethics. Thus the professional is an educated, skilled, institutional and responsible person who gains respect and social status through competence and the possession of esoteric knowledge (Campbell 1985, 25).

Now if the purpose of the Church is defined as "the increase among men (*sic*) of the love of God and neighbour" (Niebuhr 1956, 31) – at first sight a very laudable aim – then it follows that:

> the work that lays the greatest claim to (the minister's) time and thought is the care of a church, the administration of a community that is directed toward the whole purpose of the church. (*ibid*, 83)

Ministry, thus defined as the administration of a church community, is clearly "a profession" according to the criteria listed above, allowing clergy to be seen as "pastoral directors" (Niebuhr 1956, 79) and their job as delineated by their public tasks, competencies and responsibilities, those of preaching, teaching, counselling, managing and evangelising. For many clergy, otherwise uncertain of their role in society today, the model of the minister as "the professional person" responsible for co-ordinating and administering church affairs is extremely attractive as Ian Boyd recently commented:

> It is in fact quite possible for ministers who enjoy managerial or administrative work to spend most of their time so engaged. If a lively and active congregation can be seen as an end in itself, a minister may perhaps avoid role uncertainty by throwing him or herself fully into building or maintaining just such a congregation. Providing congregational leadership is then understood as the fundamental clerical function.
>
> (Boyd 1995, 194)

Such an emphasis clearly has implications for ministerial training. If ministry can thus be seen to bear the sociological marks of a profession, then seminary training must concentrate upon skilling a candidate in the required functions and competencies. With these tasks forming the *ratio studiorum* (*qua* Gustafson 1969, 246–8 and Feilding 1966), theological education becomes little more than a shallow imparting of information and a training in the pragmatics of ministry. Thus Leech can say:

> Training for ministry comes to be increasingly taken up with the acquisition of skills in management and counselling, in the expertise necessary for efficient control of the institution, and for efficient handling of personal problems.
>
> (Leech 1989, 129)

A damning indictment, but one which is echoed by numerous other commentators (Holmes 1976b, 138; Thomas 1969, 346; Lindbeck 1996, 295).

Edward Farley would likewise agree that the prevailing ethos in Western theological schools is that of professionalism. In this incisive critique of theological education (Farley 1982) he charts the course of theological study from an initial grounding in sapiential knowledge of God, through a period in which it is seen both as a product of divine illumination and as a science, to the current situation characterised by the loss of *theologia* and its dispersion into independent disciplines whose end and unity is training for ministerial tasks. Such a dispersion is largely attributed to two movements in human cultural and religious life: those of continental pietism and the Enlightenment, the latter introducing modes of thought into culture, education and religion which are still very much with us today. The rationalist-materialist-reductionist paradigm within which theological education still largely operates (Drane 1995, 3) is a direct legacy of Enlightenment thinking, as is the equation of education with the ideals of objectivity, fact and theory, and our current understanding of it as an essentially cognitive act (Bridges-Johns 1997, 135). *Theologia's* fate, Farley concludes, is to have become merely the personal knowledge – worse still, the technological knowhow – required for the institutional and administrative task of ministry, whilst theological education has mutated into "theological training", the latter word implying "that there is a fixed content and a fixed methodology, both of which need to be communicated" (Rogers 1982, 356).

Disquiet has, however, been raised on several fronts regarding such a trend. Many in the field of pastoral care, for instance, point to the limitations of professionalism when faced with the open-ended, risky messiness of so much Christian loving. How can one set boundaries when called to seek and serve those who, like Him, suffer outside the gate? (Leech 1997, 231–6; Campbell 1985 passim; 1991, 37). Others point to the danger of "religious organisers" being so sucked in to serving the Church's needs as to be both uncritical and unprophetic (Boyd 1995, 194; Fiorenza 1996, 337).

My unhappiness with the inadequacy of the professional model goes deeper than that. To see why, we must return to Niebuhr's definition, one which has enjoyed a wide currency over the years. There ministry was defined as "the administration of a community *whose purpose is the increase among men of the love of God and neighbour*" (Niebuhr 1956, 83). Steven Mackie's criticism is both acute and concise;

> This seems to me altogether too subjective and too limited a conception, omitting as it does any reference to what God has achieved in Christ, to the hope which he has given his people and to the work of the Spirit in their midst. It leads easily into an

understanding of the church's intention as solely and sufficiently expressed in voluntary societies of like-minded folk.

(Mackie 1965, 84)

The Church surely has a much wider and more glorious calling than Niebuhr allows, namely to be a sign and a sacrament to all humanity of God's redemptive work in creation. Every member of the body has a God-given ministry to point to God's ultimacy and sovereignty, to articulate a sense of the sacred in a relative world, to mediate His presence and action. "You are a royal priesthood, a dedicated nation, a people claimed by God for His own, to show forth the excellencies of the One who called you." (IPet 2, 9) Ministry is the task of communicating the truth, of offering people a "transcendent reference" for their lives (Carr 1985, 17), of expanding their awareness; it is a vocation to mystagogy, a calling to act as guardian and guide of insight and mystery, awakening others to the reality of God.

By their lives ministers exhibit the transcendent dimension of God's love. They are charismatic, liminal, even strange people, "not professionals like any other professionals, but *"extraordinary people"* (Westerhoff 1982, 163). To describe ministry in these terms is to see it not as a job or an assumed role as hitherto – not to define it pragmatically in terms of function – but rather as an identity; in other words, the emphasis shifts from tasks and skills to character and inwardness, from doing to being. As was said of the Desert Father, St Anthony, after twenty years' solitude in Pispir, *"his entire being was ministry"* (Nouwen 1981, 32).

The nurture of ministers

Reconceiving ministry as the task of pointing to the relationship between God and humanity, and ministers as the agents of that illumination, has implications for the curricula of theological schools. Under the professional paradigm, theological education was seen largely as a cognitive pursuit; there was a fixed body of information which was imparted to students by means of a "banking" (Freire 1982, 45–7) or "jug" (Drane 1995, 4) pedagogy. The philosophy of Christian growth underlying such methods was that imbibing a certain amount of biblical exegesis and doctrinal theology brought about maturity in Christ; godly learning, in other words, made for godly people, the very reductionism of the Reformed tradition which Edwin Muir castigates in *The Incarnate One* (Muir 1991, 213).

The training of ministers as mystagogues and liminal people requires a shift from a technological, functionalist view of education to a much more Brodie-esque approach. In this regard the ancient Greek ideal of education as a "culturing" of human beings may be of help: education as the process whereby a person is shaped and affected by virtue (here, sapiential knowledge of God), education as the development of the whole person rather than merely as the acquisition of knowledge, education which develops a person affectively as well as cognitively. The type of education which so transfigures a person that they are brought to the point – via wilderness and cross – of saying "it is no longer I who live but Christ who lives in me" (Gal. 2, 20).

This is not to deny the need for competence and expertise. There *are* skills and techniques needed in the exercise of ministry; knowledge of the tradition *is* important. But ministerial training is first and foremost a matter of formation, the development of character, spiritual ascesis; it is primarily concerned with fostering a student's attentiveness to God. "It is the acquisition of an instinct, a taste for God" (Mason 1994, 160).

This is not to suggest that ministerial learning is some sort of anti-incarnational pursuit – the term "formation", alas, often conjures up such misconceptions (Holmes 1976b, 137–8); indeed the intention here is quite the reverse. In *The Sovereignty of Good* Iris Murdoch commented that "it is a *task* to come to see the world as it is" (Murdoch 1970, 91) and it is this *task*, this rigorous vocation, which lies at the heart of the type of formation here proposed. Ministers must be helped on the one hand to imbibe the disciplines of prayer, meditation, *lectio devina*, silence, repentance, vision and discernment, disciplines which will enable them to know God as the ground of all being, and on the other to be fluently conversant with the language, literature and tradition of the Church through the ages. But more importantly they must be helped to become the kind of people *who can bring these two elements together*, and so enable others to engage in the same creative dialetic in their own lives.

In essence the chief task of theological educators is to form *reflective practitioners* of the faith. It is not our job to provide students with a corpus of prepackaged theological judgements or "answers to antici-pated questions" (Mason 1994, 159–60), but rather to furnish them with the capacity to make those judgements and answer those ques-tions from the depths of their own beings, "to encourage them to be theologians for themselves" (Williams 1996, 23). The task is so to foster a close relationship with God and a deep knowledge of the Christian mythos that they are enabled to interpret situations in the lives of others, helping them to discern in them dimensions of corruption and dissonance with divine will, as well as signs of hope and redemptive possibility, and so move towards renewed understanding and trans-formative action. It is to lead students towards a ministry of interpretation and mediation, of evocation and facilitation.

Formation should enable ministers to engage in constant theological reflection, defined by Durston as "the process of relating experience in the contemporary world and the Christian heritage of faith so as to discern God's presence and action in a way that leads to renewed atti-tudes or action" (Durston 1989, 35). Such training should enable them to make meaningful syntheses of the tradition and the actuality of people's experience so that "lives are illumined in a new way by God's vision for his creation" (Holmes 1978, 7). In this way the ministry of the *entire* Christian community may be unleashed and mobilised towards redemptive activity in the world.

But in order to make connections between these elements of revelation, two characteristics must be fostered during the formation process. The first I shall call "sensibility", a receptive dexterity of the soul, a capacity for open-minded and wide-eyed attention. It is an act of developing an I-Thou relationship with reality, of participating in the significance of the "sacramental universe" in which we live (Temple 1940, 473), rather than adopting a heavy-handed literalist approach and treating objects as mere means to an end. It is the ability to "see a world in a grain of sand" (Blake: *Auguries of Innocence*), to sense that we live on holy ground.

Poets are particularly gifted in achieving an immediate experience of phenomena and creating new insights from such responsiveness, as can be seen from the following excerpt from T.S. Eliot's 1921 essay, *The Metaphysical Poets*;

> When a poet's mind is perfectly equipped for its work, it is constantly amalgamating disparate experience; the ordinary man's experience is chaotic, irregular, fragmentary. The latter falls in love, or reads Spinoza, and these two experiences have nothing to do with each other, or with the noise of the typewriter or the smell of cooking; in the mind of the poet these experiences are always forming new wholes.
>
> (Eliot 1969, 287)

So also in the mind of ministers; the different loci of divine epiphany of the sacred Story and the particular narratives of everyday life should likewise be so conjoined – Foskett and Lyall liken the process to intercourse 1988, 50) – that *new wholes are formed*, new possibilities revealed.

The second characteristic which must be fostered is the capacity to be at ease with risk, a willingness to renounce mastery and control, security and comfort, and live instead in the wilderness, "on the threshold between structure and anti-structure" (Holmes 1976, 221). As Christ called His disciples to lead lives of self-denial (Mk 8, 34), insecurity (Mk 6, 8) and servanthood (Mk 10, 44), subverting the rationality and prudent standards of His day, so too are ministers called to die to the world's notions of control and success and be at home instead in the realms of powerlessness, ambiguity, spontaneity and risk. For only there will they be able to "grow towards the future" (Holmes 1971, 218), only there will they be in touch with new possibilities, new revelations of God.

The world desperately needs women and men graced with sensibility and at ease with uncertainty who can point to the transcendent and awaken a sense of the divine. As a character in Iris Murdoch's novel *The Good Apprentice* cries, "we need priests, we miss them and will miss them more, *we miss their power*" (Murdoch 1986, 69). But have theological schools trained people to be this kind of powerful liminal figure? I think not. Yet the literature is littered with hints as to how seminaries might do so. Holmes comments that "authentic ministry must have at its centre the person who is above all an artist" (Holmes 1971, 222), Drane calls for "more right-brained or creative experiences" (Drane 1995, 5), Wood for the development of "sensitivity and imagination" (Wood 1985, 90), Campbell for the nurturing of "creativity and sensitivity" and "the rekindling of the imagination" (Campbell 1985, 76; 1991, 98) and Chopp for a "reinvigoration of the imagination" (Chopp 1990, 121) – all seemingly calling for more attention to be paid to the imagination. To see whether the development of this faculty would indeed help form the type of minister described above, we must first examine the nature and workings of the imagination.

Imagination: The Spark of the Spirit

Redeeming the imagination

> Imagination, a licentious and vagrant faculty, unsuceptible of limitations and impatient of restraint.
>
> (Samuel Johnson. *The Rambler*)

From the time of Aristotle until the middle of this century, the imagination has had a bad press. The venom of Dr Johnson's critique is matched by Luther's commentary upon Genesis 8, verse 21, in which imagination is viewed as the seat of human evil (Schick 1960, 122), and by Calvin's splenetic diatribe against "presumptuous imaginations" which lead people astray (Troeger 1990, 106). Not only has this great faculty been seen as the opponent of godly living, acquiring for itself a "shady reputation" (Jennings 1976, 11), but it has also become synonymous in common parlance with the antithesis of reason and relegated to the realms of illusion, fantasy and unreality. We in the West have been schooled to regard intuition, imagination and creativity as inferior to, and separate from, intellect, reasoning and the more theoretical of rational processes. In a world of left-brained dominance, we have learned to live with our heads alone, eschewing the heart. The unity of Wordsworth's "feeling intellect" (Warnock 1976, 128) has been replaced by Barfield's "islanded consciousness" (Jennings 1976, 12).

Andrew Louth in *Discerning the Mystery* (Louth 1983) traces this "dissociation of sensibility" (Eliot 1969, 288) back to the scientific advances of the seventeenth century and the Enlightenment's search for objective truth via scientific method. Until scientific rationality's self-confident edifice began to totter in recent decades, such an experimental method for establishing objective truth, predicated upon the tenets of verifiability, repeatability and quantifiability, was considered paradigmatic for all human knowing. The growth of the historical-critical method of textual analysis is but one example of the fevered adoption of such a methodology by theology. Objectivity became the highest accolade bestowable upon thought, and imagination, by contrast, was pilloried as an inferior and unreliable source of knowledge (Brueggemann 1997, 32).

For too long theology has eschewed associating with the imagination, believing that such a union could only be "damaging to (its) reputation" (Jennings 1976, 11). But as Saint-Exupéry so clearly demonstrates in his fable exposing the absurdity of scientific rationalism, *The Little Prince* (Exupéry 1982), "unless (we) turn round and become like children" (Matt 18, 3), unless we allow ourselves to think associatively as well as literally (Holmes 1976a, 104), we will continue to be hard-hearted, unable to engage with the Truth; the mysteries of God will, alas, remain as propositional formulae.

From the middle of this century, however, the tide has been turning with consideration of the imagination gradually regaining its rightful place at the heart of the theological endeavour. John Baillie's *cri de coeur* triggered off research by other Scottish theologians (McIntyre 1986; 1987; Mackey 1986) and latterly the field has become even wider (Tracy 1981; Fischer 1983; Grey 1997):

> I have long been of opinion (*sic*) that the part played by the imagination in the soul's dealings with God … has never been given proper place in Christian theology, which has too much been ruled by intellectualist preconceptions. (Baillie 1941, 77)

Such a move must be set against the rehabilitation of the imagination which has occured in a multitude of disciplines other than theology, a development which, for clarity's sake may be set under two heads. First came the rediscovery of the cognitive claims of imagination, denied since the classical period, the realisation that the imagination was not a single isolable faculty of the mind but rather "the whole mind working in certain ways" (MacIntyre 1987, 159). As Walter Brueggemann puts it, imagination has made an important comeback as "a reliable mode of knowledge" (Brueggemann 1997, 32). Far from it being the possession of only a few gifted individuals, it is now clear that the imagination is a faculty "common to all human beings" (Warnock 1986, 155), a "fundamental human ability" (Walsh in McIntyre 1986, 121) basic to every part of the cognitive enterprise. No longer can it be seen merely as an optional intellectual extra, peripheral to the main business of knowing, living and working; rather do we "depend on it for our definition of reality" (Troeger 1990, 100).

As such it has a wide brief, best summarised in the following excerpt from Mary Warnock's seminal study of 1976:

> (The imagination) is at work in our everyday perception of the world, and is also at work in our thoughts about what is absent; (it) enables us to see the world, whether present or absent, as significant, and also to present this vision to others, for them to share or reject. And this power, though it gives us "thought-imbued" perception, is not only intellectual. Its impetus comes from the emotions as much as from the reason, from the heart as much as from the head.
>
> (Warnock 1976, 196)

Such an analytic of the imagination sees it performing a number of roles. As the image-forming faculty, it provides the capacity for recognising and making sense of the world around us as well as bringing to mind objects of perception by means of memory and recall; in other words it both "presents and represents" reality to us (*ibid*, 102). Added to this it enables us to perceive the world "as significant of something familiar" (*ibid*, 10), and to communicate that understanding to others. Scholars have since added to this list of "seeing-as" functions, with Eslinger extending the scope from the purely visual mode to include "imagining-that" and "imagining-how" (Eslinger 1995, 60) and McIntyre proposing an even lengthier analytic of twelve functions (McIntyre 1987, 159–68).

The second principal factor in the rehabilitation of the imagination has been the realisation across a multiplicity of disciplines that all human conceptual systems are metaphoric in nature; in other words there has been an appreciation of the "creative, interpretive character of human existence" (McFague 1987, 22). In the construal of reality we rely on metaphor or else upon models, "systematically developed" forms of metaphor (Mackey 1986, 6). As McFague writes:

> there is no such thing as a value-free, neutral, direct route to reality; if we are to have any knowledge of reality at all, it must be heavily dependent on models.
>
> (McFague 1983, 99)

Thus in the realm of faith, since the Infinite is only revealed through the finite, to speak of God's being necessitates the use of analogy, to speak of His action, myth (or "imaginative narrative"; Knox 1964). Faith is necessarily imagistic and symbolic, for the real God is never directly knowable by us.

Now while theology has been content to acknowledge this – witness the immense current interest in narrative and metaphorical theology on both sides of the Atlantic – more surprising has been the scientific community's admission of its debt to the metaphoric, intuitive and symbolic knowledge (Bausch 1991, 24; Fischer 1982, 2). The narrow positivist view of science detailed above is now outmoded, and instead there is appreciation of the centrality of models in both theory and practice. Models depend on "as-if" (imaginitive) thinking; they are heuristic devices, "imaginative constructs invented to account for observed phenomena" (Barbour in McIntyre 1987, 130), the creation of which requires "a special kind of creative imagination" Mackey 1986, 6). This is a hearty endorsement of the role of imagination in science; imagination, at long last, is being "judged adequate to deal with reality" (McFague 1983, 91).

But Paul Ricouer has pushed the importance of the imagination in the construal of reality even further, pointing to its *creative function* in the generation of knowledge. He conceives of metaphors as semantic imaganitive acts which conjoin contradictory meanings, and by this act of collision thereby create new meanings. Ricouer asks:

are we not ready to recognise in the power of imagination, no longer the faculty of deriving "images" from our sensory experience, but the capacity for letting new worlds shape our understanding of ourselves? This power would not be conveyed by images, but by the emergent meanings in our language. Imagination would thus be treated as a dimension of language.

(Eslinger 1995, 68–69)

Imagination is thus no longer construed as primarily *re*productive as in Warnock's definition, but as *pro*ductive of new meaning. Such a way of understanding the imagination is nothing less than "a new way of languaging and engaging in meaning" (Murray in Eslinger 1995, 115). High claims indeed, and far removed from the dismissive comments with which this chapter began!

Imagination as the connecting force

Mature as he was, she might yet be able to help him to the building of the rainbow bridge that should connect the prose in him with the passion. Only connect! That was the whole of her sermon.

(E.M. Forster   *Howards End*   Chapter XXII)

In the foregoing attempt to demonstrate the centrality of the imagination in all forms of thinking, many of the faculty's roles and functions were touched upon. To describe each of these in turn would be impossible in a project of this size; for that the reader is referred to the epistemological studies of Ray Hart, John McIntyre, David Tracy, James Mackey and Kathleen Fischer (Hart 1968; McIntyre 1987; Tracy 1981; Mackey 1986; Fischer 1983). Here one role only will be isolated from imagination's vast repertoire, that of "making connections".

Though such an understanding of the imagination as "an active combining power" (Warnock 1976, 84) might appear to be a recent development, underpinning as it does the linguistic-semantic theory of Ricouer and other philosophers of language, nevertheless its roots lie far beneath the topsoil of structuralism. The Romantic poet and literary commentator Samuel Taylor Coleridge devoted much of his *Biographia Literaria* (1817) to an account of the imagination, envisaging it as having an active and creative role in bringing together "disparate or opposite materials", a task to which he applied the ugly epithet "esemplastic". In Chapter XIV of that work he describes the poet's work in the following way:

He diffuses a tone and spirit of unity ... by that synthetic and magical power to which we have exclusively appropriated the name of imagination. This power, first put into action by the will and understanding, reveals itself in the balance or reconciliation of opposite or discordant qualities.

(Warnock 1963, 93)

Later in *The Statesman's Manual* he describes imagination as "that reconciling and mediating power … with which we actively bring together different perceptions" (*ibid*, 100). Wordsworth perceived the imagination in similar fashion; in a fragment of poetry written in 1798, he too speaks of the imagination as the *combining power*. Nor is it only poets who have conceived of the imagination in this way. The physicist Jacob Bronowski has written as follows:

> The world is totally connected. The act of imagination is the opening of the system so that it shows new connections.
>
> (Bronowski 1978, 109)

Others speak of it as a "bridge" (Fischer 1983, 7) or even a "rainbow bridge" as in the quotation from *Howards End* above; alas, there, Henry's "obtuseness" (Forster 1989, 188) prevented him from making any such connections!

There would thus appear to be a concensus of opinion across several disciplines that the imagination is the brain working analogically, bringing into association disparate ideas thus giving birth to hitherto unknown possibilities; by the making of such metaphoric connections, new visions are created, new insights formed, new solutions reached. The homiletician Paul Scott Wilson graphically likens this process to the electric spark which jumps between the charged poles of a hand-cranked telephone generator when they are a certain distance apart (Wilson 1988, 33–4; 1995, 245).

Bishop J.V. Taylor in *The Go-Between God* and *A Matter of Life and Death* likewise compares the Holy Spirit to a spark, a "current of charged intensity" (1986, 3) passing between two people, or between man and nature, creating moments of annunciation, revelation, heightened awareness. Rather than personalising this expression of God's Being, Taylor characterises the Spirit as an energy – "the elemental energy of communion itself" (1992, 18), that process which enlivens us and opens the doors of perception; he writes:

> every time I am given (such) unexpected awareness towards some other creature and feel this current of communication between us, I am touched and activated by something that comes from the fiery heart of the divine love, the eternal gaze of the Father towards the Son, of the Son towards the Father (*ibid*, 18).

This animator and energiser of life is at work anonymously within <u>every</u> human being. Some may choose to ignore or resist its promptings, finding such aliveness too painful; like Forster's Henry, they thus become "estranged from the life which is in God through the incomprehension that is in them through the stony hardness of their hearts" (Eph 4, 18). Others, on the other hand, may "lower the barriers"

(Taylor 1986, 13) and choose life, plugging themselves ever more fully into the current of communication.

It is my contention that the action of the Spirit – this power that makes connections between the extraordinary and the ordinary in our lives, that rouses us into being aware of the Infinite in the finite – is identical to that of the imagination; that the imagination, in other words, is the spark of the Spirit. Both awaken us to be creatively receptive to conditions around us and responsive to new possibilities, to spark us into that fullness of life (John 10, 10) for which we were all created, to *inspire* us to new vision. Both can awaken us to be disciples of Him who was supremely aware of life around Him, a person of "extraordinary creative imagination" (Boff 1980, 90) who refused to be hidebound by convention but was constantly open to the promptings of the Spirit, gloriously aware, ever awake to the new.

The Spirit, I believe, is present in all who are made in the image of God (Taylor 1986, 11), and has been since the dawn of creation (Gen 1, 2; Ps 104, 30; Job 33, 4); throughout history, She has been drawing the whole created universe to awareness of what is and what is to be, albeit refracted through a Christological lens since the Incarnation (Taylor 1992, 107). In short, the Spirit is a universal human gift, just as the imagination is a universal human faculty. Thus such events as "the coming of the Spirit" at the Jordan or at Pentecost, or to believers nowadays, rather than being moments of *addition* are moments of reorientation, of metanoia, of deepening awareness of this presence already within us, of "being what we are".

Such a comparison between Spirit and imagination is not new; Coleridge termed the imagination the "repetition in the finite mind of the eternal act of creation in the infinite I AM" (Troeger 1990, 114), while McIntyre likewise argues that "the Holy Spirit's characteristic activity is imaginitive creation in the spirits of believers" (McIntyre 1987, 64; see also O'Donoghue 1993, 85–6; Bailey 1996, 65; Maitland 1995, 109). Here, however, I would like to push it further. For though all may possess the Spirit/imagination in some form, clearly some imaginations are more creative than others, just as some people are more alive to the Spirit than others. How then is this power nurtured? How do we so stimulate our imaginations that the current may even spark brightly, making us aware of and alive to "God in all things"?

I would argue that the answer to that question, posed in those different ways of languages, lies in the development of a sacramental spirituality in which everything is seen as a bearer of meaning, a sign of transcendence, a door to the sacred. Everything in creation, in its essence, testifies to its Creator; humanity may mar and deform that image by perpetrating sin, but beneath that, could we but hear it, all "creation praises its master" (Barth in Harries 1993, 146). And the people who can best help us towards such a sacramental feeling for life are not saints and martyrs, the conventional holy people, but poets.

Scots are used to calling poets "makars", those who form new bodies of imaginative response, co-creators with Him who is Maker of all. By and large however poets find "no place as yet among those commemorated in our churches as prophets and teachers and lights of the world in their several generations" (Ecclestone 1990, 56). Yet they are those whose very lives are attuned to watchful attention, to noticing the minutiae of creation, to experiencing phenomena in an immediate fashion; they are those who cultivate in themselves and in their readers what Barfield calls the "tender receptiveness of the heart" (Holmes 1971, 218). They are those who testify to the holy in the habitual, forming fresh epiphanies with words.

From such watchful attention they amalgamate disparate experiences to form new wholes: falling in love and reading Spinoza, the evening with a patient on an operating table, lovers in bed and a pair of compasses. Refusing to let their minds be imprisoned by the humdrum and the clichéd, they "stand in the place where the rules are different" (Maitland 1995, 143), and from that experience of liminality create new descriptions of reality. And by these acts of cleansed perception their readers are enabled to see with a new intensity into the heart of the matter, to discern the "inscape" (to use Hopkins' word); by their art we are "quickened", made more alive and receptive.

It is my contention that those who seek to help others find the Transcendent in their lives have much to learn from poets; we must listen to them, emulate the limpid way they notice the ordinary, and cultivate the same boldness in making connections. We must immerse ourselves in their work until our mindsets too become poetical, our Spirits and imaginations untrammeled by dullness and obduracy. Then will we be alive to the truth and glory of God in the everyday, and able to communicate that to others. As we train ourselves to encounter the Word in suprising new contexts – unchurchy, secular, ordinary contexts – and convey these associations to others, our ministries will come alive; they will become more akin to the exuberant, risky celebration of faith that Maitland longs for in the following lyrical passage:

> We need jugglers and high-wire artists – sequinned, sparkling and dancing on the void – if theology is to measure up at all to the magnificent God whose gambling habits and sleights of hand boggle our simple minds. We need a deeply imaginitive meditation on the narratives and symbols of our past if we hope to co-create a future. We need a powerful vision of the beauty of God and the beauty of Her creation; not false prophets who cry peace, peace when there is no peace; but those who will ride the wild storm cloud and hide in the clefts of the rock just to see the hinderparts of God.

> (Maitland 1995, 145)

But not only will such a theology be in love with playfulness and risk; it will also be deeply prophetic and countercultural. Just as "new metaphors have the power to create a new reality (which) becomes deeper when we begin to act in terms of it" (Lakoff and Johnson 1980, 145), so too will our nurturing of the Spirit/imagination in this way bring about God's "new reality". For from such radical associations will come a reimagining of the status quo, the evoking of the alternative perceptions and subversive possibilities of the Kingdom; as Urban Holmes puts it, "to imagine is to escape the procrustean bed of the given culture's collective representation of experience (Holmes, 1976a, 104). Like Jesus, the poetic minister will refuse to "absolutise the present" (Brueggemann 1978, 119), pointing instead to the new future given by God, urging people to work for its coming on earth – the type of future "imagined" in the following lines by one in whose life poetry and priesthood have ever been intimately connected.

> It's a long way off but inside it
> There are quite different things going on:
> Festivals at which the poor man
> Is king and the consumptive is
> Healed; mirrors in which the blind look
> At themselves and love looks at them
> Back; and industry is for mending
> The bent bones and the minds fractured
> By life. It's a long way off, but to get
> There takes no time and admission
> Is free, if you will purge yourself
> Of desire, and present yourself with
> Your need only and the simple offering
> Of your faith, green as a leaf.
>
> R.S. Thomas   *The Kingdom* (1993, 233).

Developing the Imagination

Redressing the balance

> In education we have a duty to educate the imagination above all
> else
>
> (Warnock 1976, 10)

Theological education should aim to form reflective practitioners of the faith, people who are so attuned and attentive to the activity of God in their own lives that they can with ease, point others to the presence of the Transcendent in their particular life-stories. People who are graced with a receptive dexterity of the soul. One way of forming such attitudes towards life is by nurturing and feeding the Spirit/imagination, stimulating it into ever more dextrous connection-making, and for that we would do well to emulate poets, people who are skilled in paying close attention to the quiddity of matter, in revealing the inscape, in creating metaphoric connections from which new apprehensions of reality emerge. People who labour to render the ineffable and the unfathomable in beautiful form, yet who are ever aware of the inadequacy of their words, who are at ease with what Keats called "negative capability".

Curricula should thus include activities which sharpen the habits of attention and description; which develop sacramental vision by bringing students into contact with an ever-widening range of matter in which others have perceived the Divine; which encourage and develop the candidates' own creative potentials; which free them, temporarily at least, from the "aggression of fact" (Thomas 1993, 356), and permit another kind of discourse, one more in tune with the apophatic nature of the theological endeavour.

Theological education has, however, largely failed to engage in such pursuits, concentrating its energies instead upon "the impartation of information" (Lindbeck 1996, 295) or the transmission of a skills-based training; it has been "cognitively dominated" (Savage 1993, 22). Like Audrey in *As You Like It*, it has feared the poetical and stuck instead to the prose of fact. For too long it has been a left-brained activity, operating purely out of that hemisphere which functions in an analytical manner and is concerned with cognition and logic (Savage 1993, 17; Bausch 1991, 47) and has failed to draw equally upon the contributions of the right lobe, the side of "primary process thinking", which deals with non-verbal skills, perception of meaning and spatial relationships, the side which is "more aware of emotional reactions *prior* to analysis" (Holmes 1976a, 90) and from which metaphor emanates (*ibid*, 91). If training is to "affirm both the intellectual and the intuitive" (Bausch 1991, 11) and "achieve a balance between the cognitive and affective domains" (Savage 1993, 19), then much effort must be given to looking at ways in which the development of the imagination can become *a fundamental and integral part* of theological curricula; it is to that "duty" that we now turn.

An experiment reviewed

The TISEC curriculum consists of a three-year programme of lectures on biblical, doctrinal and spiritual theology, pastoral, ethical and liturgical studies, Church history and ecclesiology, mission and ministry. Such a diet of study is set against a background of corporate worship, whether in the small regional groups which meet weekly or the larger, Province-wide, gatherings at residential weekends and Summer Schools. In 1997 it was decided that the penultimate Summer School for our second tranche of students should focus upon the theme "Christianity and the Arts" and thus a fascinating week's programme was mounted, involving lectures on poetry, sacred music, Chagall and Miro, demonstrations of clowning, story-telling and the art of the haiku, the watching of the film *Babette's Feast*, and practical sessions on painting, drama and poetry. During the week, students prepared a ten-minute presentation in a medium of their choice which was then delivered on the final day. Mimes, dramatic monologues, a sculpture of leaves, meditations using newly-created paintings and poems, music, story-telling and much more was offered, a dazzling display of gifts in which hitherto unseen facets of people caught the light and sparkled.

This clearly was one way of developing student's imaginations, of stimulating the Spirit within them. But how effective had it been? Had it worked for everyone or had some remained unmoved? Would its effect be purely short-term, or would they be more pervasive than that? Was such an intensive week the best mode of delivery, or would a more extended format be preferable?

It was with these questions in mind that I devised two questionnaires which were sent to those thirteen students who had attended the School and were continuing into the final year of the course. The first, sent in October 1997, asked for "a snapshot of your reactions to some of the creative pursuits undertaken at Summer School" in an attempt to elicit immediate and not too polished responses from the participants. The second was sent six months later, by which time all had completed a lengthy parish attachment involving liturgical leadership, preaching and pastoral care, and had also been responsible for numerous acts of worship elsewhere. The aim of this set of questions was to elicit information about "the *effects* of the Summer School's input upon your practice of ministry", in particular the areas of spirituality (personal Rule of Life), preaching/teaching, liturgical ministry and pastoral praxis.

Of the thirteen students originally contacted, only one felt unable to respond to the first questionnaire; the twelve replies thus received were evenly divided between the genders. By the time the second questionnaire was sent to those same twelve, two further students, one male, one female, failed to respond, so again the genders where evenly represented. Subsequent conversations with these ten showed that *all* had treated the project as a piece of private research rather than a course evaluation and been equally keen to help, a fact of some significance as will be seen below.

What follows is a summary of the findings of these two questionnaires, distilled into tabular form. Given the small size of the sample, the reults which emerge must not be treated as conclusive "proof" of any point of view but rather as a provisional hypothesis in need of further testing on a much larger scale.

In Table 1 the horizontal rows refer to the student respondents, A to F being male, G to L female, while the vertical columns detail their most common replies, (as well as the amount of writing submitted). Such a method of presentation makes one outcome immediately clear – namely *the gender nature of the responses.*

The first questionnaire asked for peoples' reactions to the Summer School with the words "how did it feel?", seeking to elicit a very immediate, heartfelt type of answer rather than a highly cogitative and long-considered response.

The women, it would appear, were at ease with this; the majority wrote well in excess of two A4 pages and were happy to talk honestly, revealingly and movingly about their reactions. The men, on the other hand, submitted much more succinct responses, barely up to one page in length. Given that all twelve had been equally keen to be involved, and knew me equally well, I contend that such a disparity is not attributable to factors of time, interest or acquaintance but is indicative of a gendered difference in writing about feelings.

Such a conclusion is borne out by the responses themselves. As will be seen from the column marked "application", the male students discussed the *familiarity or novelty of the skills* practised during the week and their *applicability* to known or imagined parish settings; in other words, they demonstrated a very pragmatic, task-orientated approach. This was not of such concern to the female students who spoke rather of the *sensation* of trying out these skills; many applied the epithet "risky" to the experience, describing how vulnerable and exposed they had felt throughout. The generation of this and other such emotions in the course of the week, however, was not perceived by them as a negative outcome, but rather as an essential growing or learning experience.

All the students had thoroughly enjoyed the week, finding it exhilerating, restful and totally different from the rest of the curriculum; the

Table 1. Summary of Results of Questionnaire 1

Student	play	excitement	risk	application	emotion	symbol	balance	embodied	connection	>2 pages
A	X	X					X			
B		X		X						
C		X				X	X			
D				X	X	X	X			
E				X	X	X	X	X	X	X
F		X		X						
G	X		X		X	X	X	X	X	X
H	X	X	X		X	X	X	X	X	X
I	X					X		X	X	
J	X		X	X	X	X	X	X	X	
K					X	X	X	X	X	X
L			X			X	X	X	X	X

23

setting – a spacious rural boarding school – contributed greatly to this feeling of "being on holiday." The men, by and large, applied the words "exciting" and "adventure" to the whole experience; the women, on the other hand, described it as "an opportunity to engage in childlike play", to "be a child, lost in concentrated thinking and making", play being "a trait which adults all too easily lose", testifying once again to their ability to experience – and own – feelings of vulnerability.

Both genders wrote fluently about the references to, and use made of, symbolism during the week – namely non-verbal, iconic and sacramental modes of communication, including music – perhaps reflecting their affinity for, and two years' training in, Episcopalian liturgy. Similarly there was mutual agreement about the importance of finding a balance between "the cerebral and the affective", "the practical and the intellectual", "the imaginative and the theoretical", and about the week's power to "rescue theology from the preserve of the mind" (see "balance"). Interestingly, however, the women described the effects of this harmonisation in the following ways: –

> it was an *integrating* process
> it encouraged us to be *whole* people
> I feel *whole*
> it *freed* us up
> it helped us to be more *fully in touch* with ourselves
> I *grew* and *flourished*

Comments displaying a marked coincidence in the use of dynamic and organic metaphors.

Such a divergence is even more strikingly apparent in those columns marked "embodied" and "connection". Without exception the female students spoke of how the creative, imaginative activities had allowed them to operate in their preferred mode – namely *from their own embodied experience*. Theology for them was clearly generated within a context of engagement and experience; "I meet God through experience first, and only then by thought and reason" wrote one. Similarly, several used the interesting phrase "being theological" as opposed to the more usual turns of expression "thinking theologically" or "doing theology", and indicated that they had viewed the presentation as a *disclosive practice*, the doing of which "revealed something of ourselves"; such presentations were, in the words of one, "incarnational". Many spoke of how they valued being able to use their bodies in expressing truth – and for this reason regretted the omission of dance from the week's programme. The following lyrical excerpt from one woman's writing gives a flavour of the praxis-based, embodied theology common to them all:

> For my mime to an Adrain Snell song I wore white makeup on my face and felt again the profound joy and freedom of being able to

express physically something of the truth of who God is for me. The white makeup (and I guess the action of the mime itself) was a veil through which I could try to communicate truth. Because of the veil I could risk having the confidence to reveal my true self.

Similarly the task of "making connections" was of vital importance to all six. One of the roles of those in ministry was seen to be that of helping people to find "heaven in ordinary", to regain "a sense of connectedness" in their lives between the "earthy and the transcendent" – and "the arts" were viewed as ideal means of achieving such a unity. Interestingly the latter term was used neither in an élitist nor a culturally-bound way; films and television were seen to be as vital to the task of connection-making as poetry and art, while the presence in the group of a student from Mozambique ensured that the issue of contextuality figured largely in their accounts.

In short the Summer School's stimulation of the imagination through creativity allowed these women – as never before during the course – to operate and speak in ways that were vital to their spiritual wellbeing. Feminist theologians have for long been pointing to women's "different way of knowing" (Graham 1996, 160); to how their theology is "rooted in experience" (Hampson 1996, 254), their "identity and knowledge grounded in practice" (Graham 1996, 156) and to the agential nature of their bodies in the formation and mediation of experience (Christ 1989, 14; Fischer 1995, 38). Not only do the responses to the first questionnaire testify to the centrality of such embodied or intuitional ways of knowing, but they also bear witness to another facet of women's spirituality, namely its emphasis upon "connectedness rather than separateness" (Fischer 1995, 2), upon "redeem(ing) the connections" (Grey 1993, 62) or the "re-uniting of Psyche and Eros" (Grey 1997, ch 4 *passim*). The rational cognitive theology offered by the curriculum – theology largely formed by male experience – had hitherto excluded these different perspectives.

As will be seen from Table 1 however, one man did indeed write at length about the embodied, creative and connective nature of his theology, of how the presentations were expressive of inner being "rather than coming over as a message", of how his spirituality was centred on feeling. Describing his churchmanship as charismatic evangelical, he spoke of his longing for more attention to be paid in the curriculum to the action of the Holy Spirit, "who seems to get little mention outside of set liturgical responses". The striking coincidence between his aliveness to the Spirit and the vitality of his intuitive, creative personality may lend weight to the equation ventured above between the Spirit and the imagination.

The emphasis of the second questionnaire differed markedly from that of the first, asking students to describe the *effect* that the Summer School's input had had upon their spirituality and practice of ministry

Table 2. Summary of Results of Questionnaire 2

Student	art	story	film/TV	music	poetry	metaphor	attention	encourage	feeding	>2 pages
A	X	X	X				X	X	X	X
B	X	X		X	X				X	X (service)
C	X	X	X	X	X	X	X	X	X	X
D	•	•	•	•	•	•	•	•	•	•
E	X	X			X	X	X	X	X	X (art)
F	•	X				X	X	X	X	
G	•	•	•	•	•	•	•	•	•	•
H	X	X	X	X	X	X	X	X	X	X
I	X	X		X	X	X	X	X	X	X
J	X	X	X	X	X		X	X	X	X
K	X			X	X		X	X	X	X
L	X	X		X		X	X	X	X	X

in the intervening months. As can be seen from Table 2 the responses this time did not demonstrate a marked gender difference, either in the amount submitted or the perspectives offered. All had written fluently and at length, with two of the men including material they had created during that time for use with congregations – namely a meditative service for Advent and artwork for Lent.

The demonstration of the power and properties of art, story, film, poetry and music during the Summer School had stimulated students to explore these media themselves; all had since drawn upon at least one of these resources in their ministries, and most had utilised considerably more. Story-telling and art had been widely used in pastoral encounters and spiritual guidance whilst scenes from television programmes and excerpts from films had featured in much preaching and teaching. Many had used, or written, poetry for meditative services and intercessory prayer, while one student had "experimented with writing colourful, evocative prose for a sermon". Although skilled in the use of symbolism already, several had tried developing this still further, using colour, sound, man-made objects of beauty (such as glass beads and batik) and objects from nature (pine cones, shells and wood) as "icons" in worship.

Not only had the students experimented in these ways themselves, but they had also attempted to encourage others to do likewise, enabling people to encounter God for themselves through contemporary images and the media. Two had led group sessions involving painting, while two others had encouraged its use in one-to-one settings – all to good effect. Those who had incorporated excerpts from films and novels in preaching had received enthusiastic feedback from people whose eyes had been opened "to see links" for the first time and were keen to get copies or details of the material used for their own use. One woman had experimented with such "connection-making" in tea-break conversations at work, a bold and imaginative missionary venture indeed.

The lectures and practical sessions on poetry had deepened the affinity of some for this mode of discourse, while creating for others a new love; "I see poetry now with new eyes, and actually asked for books of it for Christmas", wrote one. More particularly, however, such an emphasis during the week had had three effects. Firstly, it had alerted people to the power of words, to the need to treat them "with respect and honour, daring and imagination" (Holloway 1996, 136); "I have been challenged to use language more creatively and economically" wrote one student, adding in parenthesis "and so will be more poetic in sermons". Secondly, it had sharpened their awareness of metaphor and made them more daring in their juxtaposition of affinities – in both public and private prayer; four students revealed how their modelling of, and relationship to, God had changed as a result of the week, involving either the use of a more inclusive image or entirely new metaphors altogether. Thirdly, it had increased their powers of attention, their observation of "the physical and material", their awareness of "the sacramentality of creation"; in the words of one woman:

> my eyes have stayed wider open to God in images (naturally and humanly produced). I have allowed myself to be delighted by a wider diversity of form/texture/shape and to ascribe more of these to God-at-work through humanity.

To some this meant espousing a more contemplative spirituality, altering the pace and "colour" of their prayer life; for another it meant "a renewed use of the psalms".

One effect about which there was complete agreement was that summarised on the chart as "feeding" – namely the awareness of the importance of keeping imaginations/Spirits alive and vibrant by giving time to literature and leisure, music and art, the appreciation of beauty and the valuing of creation. Nor was this simply a pipe dream for those halcyon, post-TISEC days, but was *already* being practised – despite the pressures of combining work, family and study. Such pursuits, moreover, were seen not as optional extras as hitherto, but as *an essential part of devotional life*. As one woman put it:

> I am now committed to there being play elements in my Rule of Life; to see reading novels and going to films etc. as aspects of play in the spiritual life. In the run-up to ordination it can feel quite 'big' and 'serious', and I need to remember that God can come to me not just as the Ancient of Days but also as a child and call me out to play. Ways of working this balance out have been going to the beach, going to art galleries, playing music (loudly!) and dancing to it, watching films and discussing them with friends.

It is a passage reminiscent of the lyrical conclusion to Thomas Merton's book *Seeds of Contemplation* which begins with these words:

> What is serious to men is often very trivial in the sight of God. What in God might appear to us as 'play' is perhaps what he Himself takes most seriously.
>
> (Merton 1994, 230)

The apprehension of that truth by these trainee ministers in itself makes the week's programme worthwhile.

An experiment assessed

However laudable that outcome, a more rigorous assessment of the week's attempt to develop the students' imaginations must nevertheless be offered in an effort to answer the questions posed above concerning methodology and effectiveness. It would appear from the responses to the first questionnaire that women warmed to the creative *modus operandi* of the week; it allowed vital aspects of their spirituality to blossom, aspects which the curriculum had hitherto failed to nurture. Without wishing to be biologically deterministic – and attempting also to avoid that other evil, "the assumption of a monolithic female experience" (Welch 1990, 138) – it would appear that such an affinity for intuitive, imaginative ways of being is not simply culturally conditioned but relates rather to gendered differences in brain function; research has suggested that women's brains "are more integrated (than men's) ... and have a greater sense of relationality" (Hampson 1996, 118). It is perhaps no coincidence then that those who are currently calling for more attention to be paid to the imagination in the field of theology are predominantly women: Sallie McFague, whose plea initiated this study, Rebecca Chopp, Kathleen Fischer, Elaine Graham, Mary Grey, Sharon Welch. All these long for the emergence of imagination-filled theologies which unite "passionate caring (with) analysis, discernment and the need for action" (Grey 1997, 106) and of pastoral practices which "encourage the development of human imagination, embodiment, spirituality and conviviality" (Graham 1997, 201); theologies and praxis, in other words, which balance and harness both rational and non-rational faculties, head and heart, left and right brain.

Having noted this (possibly innate) prevalence however, I would contend on the evidence of the Summer School that it is possible to develop the imaginations of *both* genders during theological training to such an extent that the ministries of all are noticeably enhanced. This is not to force everyone into the mould of operating as "intuitives"; although research into personality types has suggested that a higher percentage of "religious leaders" takes in information through their imaginations (rather than through their senses) than is the case in the population at large (Goldsmith and Wharton 1993, 137; Goldsmith 1997, 49, 65), it must also be remembered that for many in ministry, both clergy and laity, imaginative intuition is their "less preferred function". My aim is rather to suggest that the development of that faculty, whether it be the dominant or the inferior function, is beneficial.

Scrutiny of the responses written eight months after the Summer School (supplemented by my own observations of the students during this time) suggests that such benefits were threefold. Firstly, people were made more alive, moved from the inattentive, torpor-ridden state which Eliot describes as "partly-living" to a vibrant awareness of life in all its richness, horror and beauty; in them was formed an attitude of "attention" (Weil 1969, 72; Murdoch 1970, 55), of intense (childlike) observation, the kind of responsiveness to the reality of the world around – and to the ultimate Reality – which Christ demonstrated in His ministry. The exercise of sitting in the school's grounds for a couple of hours, silently "awakening to the Real within all that is real" (Merton 1994, 2) prior to distilling the experience into a haiku that evening, or the discipline of patiently observing an object prior to painting it during another session, gazing at it with what Constable called "a humble mind" (Gorringe 1990, 120), affected people deeply, so much so that intercessory prayer and pastoral encounters were seen over the next three terms to display heightened levels of awareness of, and reverence for, the mundane and ordinary, and a resultant increase in magnanimity towards the particularity of peoples' lives.

Secondly, people were brought to a deeper understanding of the truth that "all of human culture is instinct with the divine" (Holloway 1996, 135), with a consequent widening in the range of material deemed by them to be "theologically relevant". Christianity "is the most avowedly materialistic of all the great religions" (Temple 1940, 478); it is through matter and humanity that we encounter the divine (Leech 1992, 223). A truly incarnational spirituality will thus see the works of mankind's hands as networks of revelation, as "the scaffolding of spirit" (R.S. Thomas *Emerging* 1993, 355); far from despising them, it will apprehend art, poetry, music and film as fundamentally hierophantic, an attitude captured beautifully in the following passage from Iris Murdoch's novel *The Bell* in which her central character visits The National Gallery in London:

> But the pictures were something real outside herself, which spoke to her kindly and yet in sovereign tones, something superior and good whose presence destroyed the dreary trance-like solipsism of her earlier mood. She felt that she had had a revelation. She looked at the radiant, sombre, tender, powerful canvas of Gainsborough and felt a sudden desire to go down on her knees before it.
>
> (Murdoch 1960, 192)

The students' ministries subsequent to the Summer School showed that they too had adopted such an attitude to "human culture"; sermons in particular benefited from this newly-enlarged vision, as people experimented with making connections between revelatory material in novels and films – *Vanity Fair*, *Wuthering Heights*, *The Railway Children*, *Forrest Gump* and *The Dead Poets' Society* being amongst those used – and that in scripture. From such clashes, such correlative conversations, emerged moments of parabolic subversion, examples of what Laurie Green has called "a new witness" (Green 1991, 93).

That reference to the destabilising power of parable leads us to the third and final effect of developing the imagination, namely an increase in receptivity to mystery and an attendant ease with "the wilderness of the antistructure" (Holmes 1976a, 240). The Summer School's emphasis upon symbol, silence and poetic modes of thought and discourse led people to begin embracing an apophatic theology, one in which the way to God is not via certainty, security and conceptual clarity, but the much riskier path of *un*knowing – *agnosia*. God in this tradition is "a statement beyond language / of conceptual truth" (Thomas; *Night Sky*; 1993, 334), encountered only through a process of radical purification, of liberation through disillusionment. Our false selves – all the defences, securities and idolatries which we erect to prevent us meeting God – must be shed in the desert reaches of the Dark Night, that "country of madness" (Merton 1997a, 21); only thus, stripped of human know-how and rationality, can we encounter the hidden One (Isa. 45, 15).

The task of ministry demands people who have worked through the process, who have "entered deeply into their own hearts, who have explored the wastes of their own inner desert" (Leech 1989, 28); it requires people who have died to the "controlled self of socialised, rational ego" (Holmes 1976a, 163) and who as a result are truly "opened up to God" (Mason 1992, 73). Just as Shakespeare described "the lunatic, the lover, and the poet" as being "of imagination all compact", so too must ministers be eccentric, counter-cultural characters, their lives permeated by the subversive folly of the Gospel. On the evidence of the students' ministries since the Summer School, it would appear that it is by developing the imagination that people are enabled to reject the pseudo-certainties of fact and comprehension, and embark instead upon the painful journey into the wilderness and the abyss – which is the home of spiritual maturation.

The adoption by the students of spiritualities characterised by an attentive awareness, a deepened appreciation of matter as the bearer of meaning and an ease with the mysteriousness of the Godhead became very clear to me when they met for their <u>final</u> Summer School a year later. During this time they were responsible for seven acts of worship, each of which had as its theme one of the Sacraments; no other guidelines were laid down, allowing complete freedom over form, content and manner of presentation.

The services thus devised delighted our senses of smell, hearing, touch and vision, as incense, sound (or silence), texture and symbol were variously employed throughout the week – but the most exciting element of all was the invention of new metaphors, new ways of imaging our relationship to God, to each other and to the world. We planted seeds in the earth during "The Grieving Church" liturgy; we contemplated a Cross woven from corn and grapes in "The Blessing Church" service; we thought of our own membership of the Body as we gazed at giant, multicoloured jigsaw pieces laid on the Chapel floor during "The Affirming Church" worship; we prayed for forgiveness in the act of dropping grains of incense into a thurible during that for "The Reconciling Church"; we listened as Gospel was set alongside Dostoevsky, Dylan Thomas beside Epistle, Psalm beside T.S. Eliot, and responded to the word enfleshed through mime and dance. And all through this we made links between symbol and word, between earthiness and transcendence, between liturgy and life; we encountered and responded to God in new ways, our perceptions and praxis altered irrevocably. In short it was a dazzling display of the capacity of enlivened imaginations to produce images and metaphors that are "productive of new forms of human flourishing, new visions of what it is to be human" (Chopp 1990, 121) – testimony indeed to the value of including "the development of the imagination as a major component in theological training" (McFague 1975, 105).

It was an enlivening experience, but more heartening still is the realisation that these students, now embarked upon workplace, sector or congregational ministries, do so with a desire – and a capacity – to enable people to meet and hear God in new ways, with a readiness to risk offering associations and metaphors which "play on the edges of language and bring out redefinitions of human experience" (Buttrick 1994, 66–7) and with a mission "to give rise to a church of new obedience" (Brueggemann 1997, 33). They will not be like those who "use the rotted words" (Stevens 1965, 61), whose perception is dulled by cliché, but ministers whose receptiveness of Spirit will enable moments of disclosure.

Prospects

A question of integration

> Hugh was surrounded by novels. He had little interest in those systematic theologians who never read novels and never listened to Mozart. His theological position was shaped by such figures as Dostoevsky, Hesse and Edwin Muir.
>
> (Leech 1989, 111)

Clearly the 1997 Summer School bore much fruit in the lives of all who attended it, fruit which is now being shared across Scotland. But what of future intakes of ministerial candidates? In seeking to develop *their* imaginations, should TISEC merely replicate this intensive mode of delivery, or would another method be preferable? Couched in different terms, that was a question put to the students in the second questionnaire. Their response was that such an emphasis upon creativity and intuitive thought should not simply be restricted to a single slot, but should rather run throughout the three years.

But how should this be accomplished? Clearly the constraints of timetabling do not allow for the *addition* to the programme of courses on art and poetry, music and film; the overall framework of the curriculum, validated by the Anglican Church's Ministry Division, must remain intact. Nor indeed would such an approach be educationally legitimate; as H. Richard Niebuhr observed some forty years ago:

> Theological inquiry is not something that can be added to humanistic and naturalistic studies. It needs to be constantly informed by them and to inform them. Hence also this responsibility is not met merely by the addition to theological studies of courses in the old or the new humanities – the study of literature, history and philosophy on the one hand, of culture, psychology and sociology on the other. The question is never one of adding bodies of knowledge to each other but always one of **interpenetration and conversation**.
>
> (Niebuhr 1956, 124)

Rather it is a "question of integration" (Yates 1992, 12), of *permeating the entire course* with an emphasis upon creativity, of encouraging the imagination by means of the *whole* curriculum.

Space does not allow me to suggest how this might occur in practice in all areas of the course. In the area of liturgical studies however, much has already been written in this vein, and indeed incorporated into the curriculum, (chiefly Hare Duke 1982; Green 1990), and likewise in the field of homiletics (Wilson 1988; 1995; Troeger 1990; Buttrick 1994; Eslinger 1995). Here I wish to look only at two fields, namely Formation and Pastoral Studies.

"Formation Studies" encompasses both theory and praxis; lectures and seminars on the history of spirituality run throughout the three years, while the development of the students' own spiritualities is closely monitored and guided by Personal Tutors. The centrality of formation in the curriculum can be seen from the disproportionate amount of time accorded it in the timetable; at least one fifth of every regional meeting is spent in prayer and worship – quite apart from any consideration that might be given to spirituality in that day's *teaching* programme – while the proportion of time allotted at provincial residential events is even higher.

One way of encouraging the imagination in Formation Studies might be to incorporate within both lectures and worship *a much wider range of source material* than hitherto, material which comes from the hands of poets and playwrights, novelists and painters, musicians and sculptors. All genuine art "catches, conveys and participates in ultimate reality" (Harries 1996, 48), and is thus intrinsically suitable as a springboard for theological reflection. In selecting material for students' contemplation, theological educators need to free themselves of "any narrow didacticism" (Gorringe 1995, 19) and display instead the enlarged vision exhibited by Thomas Merton in the following extract from his Journals:

> Rev. Father complained to Fr Prior about Fr John of the Cross reading the Brothers Karamazov. 'I don't see where he gets time to read 800 pages of a novel!' There is the question in a nutshell. The Brothers Karamazov is a novel. Therefore a 'temporal thing'! Therefore the time spent reading it is ipso facto without merit – a worldly and unreligious act. Whereas to read Tanquerey's Spiritual Life … that is another matter. What if it turned out that the Brothers Karamazov were really a religious book? And **what if reading it should open up new depths in our soul and make us see everything in a new light** – and perhaps realise everything is not quite so simple as devoting oneself to religious practices?
>
> (Merton 1997b, 75)

Similarly Michael Hare Duke, writing of the struggle to complete a book on the Church and communication, declares, rather delightfully;

> I was stuck until Schulz provided the inspiration with the Snoopy cartoon which appeared at the beginning of this postscript. The essence of a belief in God as Lord of the whole creation is to look for signs of his presence everywhere, to expect that connections will be made, so that insight from one quarter plays into understanding from another. **A living spirituality for me implies that**

ability to connect; so that my prayer is fed from a whole host of sources.

(Hare Duke 1982, 109)

Poetry is one such source, novels another; their handling of the themes of faith, hope, judgement and redemption is worth serious consideration. Indeed "it is in literature, as much as theology, that the profoundest exploration of these issues has been carried on" (Harries 1995, vii). How exciting it would be to see students tackling an essay on the theme of "resurrection" using not only biblical material as hitherto, but also such works as Dostoevsky's *Crime and Punishment*, Tolstoy's *Resurrection* and Eliot's *Silas Marner*. Nor need it only be "the classics" that are so used; *worthwhile contemporary fiction* should also "commend itself to the seeker after truth" (Vance 1981, 420); the works of William Golding, Anne Tyler, Sara Maitland and Thomas Eidson could all be used to good effect when either studying or praying about the themes of "journeying", "salvation", "betrayal" and "hope".

Acquaintance with such literature during training might well foster a new love, nurturing a habit to be continued into ministerial life, an outcome much to be desired. As Kenneth Leech wrote following his description of Fr Hugh Maycock quoted at the head of this chapter;

Many clergy and pastors become extremely narrow in their experience, and deficient in their imaginative faculties. 'Keep up your reading', if it is followed at all, tends to be interpreted to mean the study of theology in a fairly narrow sense. But we need to read books which will nourish the human imagination, the total person, not just inform the ecclesiastical functionary.

(Leech 1989, 111–2)

Or as the American writer on spirituality Eugene Peterson put it, "reading a novel is among the more serious activities available to a pastor" (Peterson 1997, 185).

The inclusion of a "regular and rich diet of novels, poetry and music" (Leech 1989, 112) in the training and subsequent ministries of these students is not so that they might demonstrate to their congregations how well read they are; "to use poetry, art and films simply as sermon fodder is a kind of homiletical prostitution" (Holloway 1996, 135). Rather it is in order to bring together in critical tension the two horizons – the insights of the arts and those revealed by scripture and tradition – so that from such a "fusion" (Gerkin in Graham 1996, 119) may come new ideas, perceptions and behaviour. Stimulation of the imagination in this way will indeed "lead into all truth" (John 16, 13).

But such critical-correlative hermeneutical conversations need not only be between the Word and *words*; "visual texts" could also be incorporated into the Formation Studies programme. Again theological educators need to guard against a tendency to be culturally snobbish and overly highbrow; film is an increasingly popular and pervasive medium which "take(s) the temperature of society through examination of its underside" (Marsh 1997, 29). Such a phrase describes the very stance which theologians of liberation the world over regard as seminal; clearly, then, the perspective of the cinema should be treated with some seriousness.

An experiment conducted with ten students – a viewing of Denys Arcand's 1989 film *Jesus of Montreal* followed by a discussion of "atonement" – demonstrated the value of including such material in the curriculum. The experience not only earthed consideration of that doctrine more firmly than had been the case in the previous year's Doctrinal Theology classes, provoking a more fluent and lively critique of the subject than hitherto, but was an excellent training in late twentieth century Christian apologetics; for

> attending to material of theological significance which does not derive directly from the Christian church, yet which may nevertheless be related to Christian theology's task, cannot but bring a theological interpreter face to face with the question of how "church" and "world" interrelate.
>
> (Marsh 1997, 33)

Encouraged by this, and by Marsh's own report of a similar experiment (Marsh 1993), the hope is to incorporate further films into the Formation Studies programme, using *The Piano*, *The Shawshank Redemption* or *Dead Man Walking* to lead into discussions of redemptive love, *Babette's Feast* prior to studying Eucharistic spirituality, and *Priest* or *Oscar and Lucinda* before consideration of the ministry of the wounded healer.

Further experimentation with the merging of visual images and the Word could also be attempted in the area of the group's corporate worship. While the students who come on the course are usually adept in the use of traditional materials to create foci for worship – candles, crucifixes, flowers and the like – few utilise the resources of the world's artistic heritage, and those who do so only select "religious" paintings or sculpture. Two pilot experiments attempted during Lent – placing Cecil Collins's mysterious painting *Fool and Butterfly* alongside St Paul's words in 1 Cor. 3, 18 on one occasion, and a Guardian cartoon of an ignored Big Issue seller with words from the Servant Song (Isa. 53, 1–9) on the other – showed that such fusions not only affected styles of prayer quite markedly, but also stimulated the students into trying out similar juxtapositions.

Turning to my second field of interest, namely Pastoral Studies, this likewise comprises a taught and a practical component; lectures and seminars on care, counselling, communication and ethics are supplemented by placements in congregational or sector ministry settings, affording the students practice in the approaches studied. In this area of the curriculum, however, little attention has hitherto been paid to stimulating the students' imaginations, a situation apparently repeated across Britain, and beyond; study of over one hundred North American seminaries demonstrated that "the arts" received little attention within Pastoral Studies and Ethics courses compared to the considerable emphasis so placed within homiletical, biblical and historical studies (Yates 1992, Table 3, 15).

Yet such a dearth is to be lamented, for the possession of a developed imagination is an <u>essential component</u> in the giving and receiving of pastoral care. It is my contention that this area of ministry should be viewed not as a prescriptive, propositional science but rather as a delicate relational art in which carer and cared-for explore the transformative potential of the situation under review. In this transaction, the ability to visualize and offer an alternative future *comes from the imagination/Spirit*; it is the Spirit which "opens one's eyes to see the situation differently" (Taylor 1992, 165), the "imagination which enables us to be totally open and receptive both to what is going on around us and also to what the sequel to that present situation might be" (MacIntyre 1987, 75). Thus just as preaching is increasingly being conceived of as an act of reimagination – "an offer of an image through which perception, experience and finally faith can be reorganised in alternative ways" (Brueggemann 1997, 32) – so ought pastoral care to be seen as an exercise in *reimagining the future* through the lens (at least on the carer's part) of a belief in God who is indeed "making all things new" (Rev 21, 5). Pastoral Studies courses "cannot be merely intellectual in character" (Campbell 1991a, 84), but must also involve the creative nurturing of this faculty of tender receptiveness, this imaginative openness to God's possibilities; as Alastair Campbell put it,

> the knowledge which undergirds pastoral care must have a demand for creativity at its centre. It must draw out the creativity of the learner, requiring a risking of self, imposing a cost, issuing a challenge, opening a vision. This cannot be achieved merely by adding academic subjects to a theological curriculum. It requires an overcoming of the split between intellect, emotion and imagination so often created in traditional education.
>
> (*ibid* 78)

One way of altering the existing Pastoral Studies programme so that such a blend is achieved would be to include some measure of "storytelling". In recent years theologians working in several branches of the discipline have come to realise that all experience has a narrative quality; story, in other words, is "constitutive of human identity and theological disclosure" (Graham 1996, 113). In narrative hermeneutical pastoral theology the task of the carer is envisaged as that of making sense of the client's experience by investigating the interaction between his/her particular story and "Sacred story" while retaining self-awareness. In this process, three horizons merge: the narrative identity of the counsellor, the story of the particular situation under consideration and the narrative identity of the Christian community. Or to put it slightly differently,

> the problem for theology is how the stories I am told in this age (your story), the story by which I am living (my story), and the biblical story (God's story) can be brought together in one unified intention, or be conjoined. It is the task of ministry to enable us to get our stories together.
>
> (Holmes 1976a, 177, 186)

It is thus suggested that early on in the Pastoral Studies programme students narrate the story of their lives to one another, describing the formative people, places and events therein as openly as possible; it has been my experience that in so ordering the material and reflecting on the comments of others, one is led to a new "acceptance of this complicated and muddled bundle of experiences as a possible theatre for God's creative work" (Williams 1990, 2). More importantly, however, in undertaking this risky, sometimes painful, task of vulnerable self-exposure, we become more sensitive to the embodied theologies of others, more aware of the unique importance of *their* stories, for story-telling is "a way of speaking from below the culture-bound, logical part of me" (Bailey 1996, 15), a way of speaking with the mind in the heart, of engaging the imagination.

In attempting this task the students will once again need to be exposed to a "rich diet" of literature, to the stories of others, be they biblical, biographical or fictional characters; for as Urban Holmes pointed out,

> the reason we find it difficult to identify our story is that we have not been fed a diet of consistent stories. If there is no literature, or if the literature is banal pap, or if it is fragmented and distorted, then we suffer from the impoverishment of the stuff of stories. Our vision is distorted because of our limited imagery.
>
> (Holmes 1976a, 185–6)

Thus as well as telling their own stories, students should be encouraged to *study the stories of others*; Margaret Forster's novels have already been cited as one such source, while the works of Iain Banks and William McIlvanney might be recommended for students embarking on ministry in a Scottish context. By so doing they will "deepen and retain the habit of story in (their) conversation and proclamation" (Peterson 1997, 188) and thus be better mediators of pastoral care.

The value of the telling and reading of "stories" here advocated is made abundantly clear in the following delightful anecdote by the American novelist Katherine Paterson:

> I was once very much involved with a young man who, when I tried to share with him my love for C.S. Lewis's Chronicles of Narnia, said earnestly that he felt it was wrong of Lewis to distort the Bible in this way. I should have known at that moment that the relationship was doomed. Aslan is not a distortion but a powerful symbol of the Lion of Judah, which can nourish our spirits as the reasoned arguments of a thousand books of theology can never do. We can dare face the dark, because we've had a shining glimpse of the light.
>
> (Paterson 1995, 70)

Perhaps the amendments to the Pastoral Studies course suggested here will so nourish the students' imaginations/Spirits that they too can help others face the dark and glimpse the Light.

Training God's spies

> Music, poetry, painting, sculpture, architecture are disciplines
> employing the equivocal symbols that live in the 'cracks'
> of our social structures and create images of the future for us.
> Life without the arts is doomed to the hell of the positivist,
> untouched by the possibility of a new order.
> We in the Church are salesmen for a new order.
> (Holmes 1971, 263)

Having discussed the merging of the three horizons which occurs in narrative, hermeneutical pastoral theology – "mine, yours and God's" – Urban Holmes goes on to outline the point of it all, namely "that a conjoining of visions emerges, through which the Spirit can move to confront us with the future" (Holmes 1976a, 190). Such a confrontation, I venture to suggest, is what nurturing the imagination of students on a theological course is all about. We are indeed training people to be "salesmen" – and women – "for a new order", God's new order.

As Kenneth Leech emphasises throughout his writing, the symbol of the Kingdom of God lies at the heart of the Gospel – it is "the regulative principle of theology" (Leech 1989, 36; 1992, 215), "the core metaphor for a new social imagination" (Leech 1997, 203); mankind is called to recognise, and co-operate with, this divine work of transformation in the midst of history. But the Kingdom is a mystery (Mark 4, 11), and thus it is the task of those who strive to serve God to

> take upon's the mystery of things
> As if we were God's spies.
>
> (King Lear Act V; sc. 3)

All spies, however, require training – and God's spies need their vision sharpened, their imaginations/Spirits enlivened, otherwise "they may look and look, but see nothing; they may listen and listen, but understand nothing" (Mark 4, 12). In order to see the signs of the Kingdom clearly, in order to be able to "dream dreams" and inspire others with the same, God's spies need "liberated imaginations" (Middleton and Walsh 1995, 192) and rejuvenated Spirits (Acts 2, 17–8). The task of theological education is thus to equip men and women *appropriately* for God's secret service.

At the time of writing another intake of ordinands and candidates for lay ministry is about to embark on the three year course. If some of the suggestions outlined above regarding such "appropriate training" are implemented, then these new students' experience will differ markedly from that outlined at the beginning of this dissertation. They will have the time and the energy *throughout* the course to read poetry and novels, go to concerts and the cinema, draw, write or paint – in short, exercise their imaginations – for such activities will be viewed as integral parts of their formation, vital to their becoming "stewards of the mysteries of God" (1 Cor 4, 1).

BIBLIOGRAPHY

Astley, J., Francis, L.J. and Crowder, C. (eds) (1996) *Theological Perspectives on Christian Formation. A Reader on Theology and Christian Education* Eerdmans/Gracewing

Bailey, S. (1996) *The Well Within. Parables for Living and Dying* DLT

Baillie, J. (1941) *Our Knowledge of God* Oxford University Press

Ballard, P. and Pritchard, J. (1996) *Practical Theology in Action. Christian Theology in the Service of Church and Society* SPCK 1996

Bausch, W. (1991) *Storytelling, Imagination and Faith* Twenty-Third Publications

Begbie, J. (1992) "The Gospel, the arts and our culture" pps 58–83 in Montefiore, H. ed *The Gospel and Contemporary Culture* Mowbray

Boff, L. (1980) *Jesus Christ, Liberator* SPCK

Boyd, I.R. (1995) "What are the clergy for? Clerical role uncertainty and the state of theology" pps 187–196 in *Theology* XCVIII no. 783

Bridges-Johns, C. (1997) "From Babel to Pentecost: The renewal of theological education" pps 132–146 in Pobee, J. ed *Towards Viable Theological Education* WCC Publications

Bronowski, J. (1978) *The Origins of Knowledge and Imagination* Yale University Press

Brown, D. and Loades, A. (1995) "Introduction: the dance of grace" pps 1–16 in Brown, D. and Loades, A. eds *The Sense of the Sacramental. Movement and Measure in Art and Music, Place and Time* SPCK

Brueggemann, W. (1978) *The Prophetic Imagination* Fortress Press (1997) *Cadences of Home. Preaching among Exiles* Westminster/John Knox

Buttrick, D. (1994) *A Captive Voice. The Liberation of Preaching* Westminster/John Knox

Campbell, A.V. (1991a) *Paid To Care? The Limits of Professionalism in Pastoral Care* SPCK (1991b) *Rediscovering Pastoral Care* DLT

Carr, W. (1985) *The Priestlike Task. A Model for Developing and Training the Church's Ministry* SPCK

Chopp, R. (1990) "Emerging issues and theological education" pps 106–124 in *Theological Education* vol 26

Christ, C.P. (1989) "Embodied thinking. Reflections on feminist theological method" pps 7–15 in *Journal of Feminist Studies in Religion* vol 5 (no. 1)

Dillenberger, J. (1986) *A Theology of Artistic Sensibilities. The Visual Arts and the Church* SCM

Drane, J. (1995) "Theological education for the next century" pps 3–8 in *British Journal of Theological Education* vol 6 no. 3

Durston, D. (1989) "Theological reflection: definitions, criteria" pps 32–39 in *British Journal of Theological Education* vol 3 no. 1 (1990) "Theological reflection – historic faith in dialogue with contemporary experience." pps 36–47 in *British Journal of Theological Education* vol 3 no. 3

Ecclestone, A. (1990) *Yes To God* DLT

Eliot, T.S. (1969) *Selected Essays* Faber and Faber

Eslinger, R.L. (1995) *Narrative and Imagination. Preaching The Worlds That Shape Us* Fortress Press

Farley, E. (1983) *Theologia. The Fragmentation and Unity of Theological Education* Fortress (1996) "Can church education be theological education?" pps 31–44 in Astley, J., Francis, L. and Crowder, C.

Feilding, C.R. (1996) "Professional education for ministry" pps 131–75 in *Theological Education* vol 3 no. 1

Fischer, K.R. (1983) *The Inner Rainbow. The Imagination in Christian Life* Paulist Press (1995) *Women at the Well. Feminist Perspectives on Spiritual Direction* SPCK

Forster, E.M. (1989) *Howards End* Penguin

Foskett, J. and Lyall, D. (1990) *Helping The Helpers. Supervision and Pastoral Care* SPCK

Freire, P. (1982) *Pedagogy of the Oppressed* Penguin

Glasse, J. (1968) *Profession: Ministry* Abingdon

Goldsmith, M. (1997) *Knowing Me, Knowing God. Exploring your spirituality with Myers-Briggs* Triangle

Goldsmith, M. and Wharton, M. (1993) *Knowing Me, Knowing You. Exploring Personality Type and Temperament* SPCK

Gorringe, T.J. (1990) *Discerning Spirit. A Theology of Revelation* SCM (1995) "Rembrandt's religious art" pps 15–19 in Theology vol XCVIII (781)

Graham, D.J. (1997) "The uses of film in theology" pps 35–43 in Marsh, C. and Ortiz, G. eds *Explorations in Theology and Film Movies and Meaning* Blackwell Publishers

Graham, E.L. (1996) *Transforming Practice. Pastoral Theology in an Age of Uncertainty* Mowbray

Green, L. (1991) *Let's Do Theology. A Pastoral Cycle Resource Book* Mowbray

Green, R. (1990) *Only Connect. Worship and Liturgy from the Perspective of Pastoral Care* DLT

Grey, M.C. (1993) *The Wisdom of Fools? Seeking Revelation for Today* SPCK (1997) *Beyond The Dark Night. A Way Forward for the Church?* Cassell

Griffiths, R. (1992) "Religion and the arts: Baudelaire and R.S. Thomas pps 5–10 in *Theology* vol XCV (763) (1997) "R.S. Thomas and the role of poetry" pps 275–285 in *Theology* vol C (796)

Gunton, C. (1991) "Mozart the theologian" pps 346–349 in *Theology* vol XCIV (761) (1992) "Knowledge and culture: towards an epistemology of the concrete" pps 84–102 in Montefiore, H. ed *The Gospel and Contemporary Culture* Mowbray

Gustafson, J.M. (1969) "Theological education as professional education" pps 243–261 in *Theological Education* vol 5 no. 3

Gutierrez, G. (1988) *A Theology of Liberation. History, Politics and Salvation* SCM

Hampson, D. (1996) *After Christianity* SCM

Hare Duke, M. (1982) *Stories, Signs and Sacraments in the Emerging Church* Mowbray

Harries, R. (1995) *Questioning Belief* SPCK (1996) *Art and the Beauty of God. A Christian Understanding* Mowbray

Hart, R.L. (1968) *Unfinished Man and the Imagination. Towards an Ontology and a Rhetoric of Revelation* Herder and Herder

Holloway, R.F. (1996) *Limping Towards the Sunrise* Saint Andrew Press

Holmes, U.T. (1971) *The Future Shape of Ministry. A Theological Projection* Seabury (1976a) *Ministry and Imagination* Seabury/Crossroad (1976b) "The strangeness of the seminary" pps 135–49 in *Anglican Theological Review Suppl. Series* vol 6

Holmes, U.T. (1978) *The Priest in Community. Exploring the Roots of Ministry* Seabury

Hopkins, G.M. (1970) *The Poems of Gerard Manley Hopkins* Oxford University Press

Hughes, K. (1997) "Conversion of mind and heart in theological education" pps 1–10 in *Theological Education* vol 33 no. 2

Isaacson, A. et al (1994) "Reflections on reflection" pps 5–15 in *British Journal of Theological Education* vol 6 no. 2

Jennings, T.W. (1976) *Introduction to Theology. An Invitation to Reflection upon the Christian Mythos* Fortress

Knox, J. (1964) *Myth and Truth. An Essay on the Language of Faith* Univ. Press of Virginia

Lakoff, G. and Johnson, M. (1980) *Metaphors We Live By* Univ. of Chicago Press

Lancelot, J. (1995) "Music as a sacrament" pps 179–185 in Brown, D. and Loades, A. eds. *The Sense of the Sacramental*

Leech, K. (1989) *Spirituality and Pastoral Care* Cowley Publications (1992) *The Eye of the Storm. Spiritual Resources for the Pursuit of Justice* DLT (1997) *The Sky is Red. Discerning the Signs of the Times* DLT

Lindbeck, G. (1996) "Spiritual formation and theological education" pps 285–302 in Astley, J., Francis, L.J. and Crowder, C.

Louth, A. (1983) *Discerning the Mystery. An Essay on the Nature of Theology* Clarendon Press

Lyall, D. (1998) "Towards a pastoral theology for modern times" pps 35–44 in *Theology in Scotland* vol V no. 1

MacIntyre, A. (1987) *After Virtue. A Study in Moral Theology* Duckworth

McDonagh, E. (1987) "Prayer, poetry and politics" pps 228–354 in Davies, B. ed *Language, Meaning and God* Chapman

McIlvanney, W. (1990) *Walking Wounded* Sceptre/Hodder and Stoughton

McIntyre, J. (1986) "New help from Kant; theology and human imagination" pps 102–22 in Mackey, J.P. ed *Religious Imagination* Edinburgh University Press (1987) *Faith, Theology and Imagination* Handsel Press

McFague, S. (1974) "Parable, metaphor and theology" pps 630–645 in *Journal of the American Academy of Religion* vol 42 (1975) *Speaking in Parables. A Study in Metaphor and Theology* SCM

McFague, S. (1983) *Metaphorical Theology. Models of God in Religious Language* SCM (1987) *Models of God. Theology for an Ecological Nuclear Age* SCM (1992) "Imaging a theology of nature: the world as God's body" pps 269–289 in Cadorette, C. *et al* eds *Liberation Theology. An Introductory Reader* Orbis

Mackey, J.P. (1986) "Introduction" pps 1–25 in Mackey, J.P. ed *Religious Imagination* Edinburgh University Press

Mackie, S.G. (1965) "Patterns of ministry and the purpose of a theological school" pps 82–88 in *Theological Education* vol 2

Macquarrie, J. (1997) *A Guide to the Sacraments* SCM

Maitland, S. (1995) *A Big-Enough God. Artful Theology* Mowbray

Marsh, C. (1993) "A feast of learning: on using film in theological education" pps 33–43 in British Journal of Theological Education vol 5 no. 2 (1997) "Film and theologies of culture" pps 21–34 in Marsh, C. and Ortiz, G. eds *Explorations in Theology and Film. Movies and Meaning* Blackwell Publishers

Mason, K. (1992) *Priesthood and Society* Canterbury Press

Merton, T. (1994) *Seeds of Contemplation* Anthony Clarke Books (1997a) *Thoughts in Solitude* Burns and Oates (1997b) *A Search for Solitude. Pursuing the Monk's True Life. The Journals of Thomas Merton vol 3 1952–60* Harper Collins

Middleton, J.R. and Walsh, B.J. (1995) *Truth Is Stranger Than It Used To Be. Biblical Faith in a Postmodern Age* SPCK

Moberly, R.C. (1910) *Ministerial Priesthood* John Murray

Muir, E. (1991) *The Complete Poems* Association for Scottish Literary Studies

Murdoch, I. (1960) *The Bell* Chatto and Windus (1970) *The Sovereignty of Good* Routledge and Kegan Paul (1986) *The Good Apprentice* Penguin

Nichols, A. OP (1980) *The Art of God Incarnate. Theology and Image in Christian Tradition* DLT

Nickoloff, J.B. (ed) (1996) "The limitations of modern theology: on a letter of Dietrich Bonhoeffer" pps 35–42 in *Gustavo Gutierrez. Essential Writings* SCM

Niebuhr, H.R. (1956) *The Purpose of the Church and its Ministry* Harper and Brothers

Nineham, D. (1993) "Epilogue" pps 186–204 in Hick, J. ed *The Myth of God Incarnate* SCM

Nouwen, H.J.M. (1981) *The Way of the Heart. Desert Spirituality and Contemporary Ministry*
DLT (1990) *The Wounded Healer* Image/Doubleday
O'Donoghue, N. (1993) *The Mountain Behind the Mountain. Aspects of the Celtic Tradition*
T. and T. Clark
Paterson, K. (1995) *A Sense of Wonder. On Reading and Writing Books for Children* Plume
Peterson, E.H. (1993) *Working the Angles. The Shape of Pastoral Integrity* Eerdmans/Grand
Rapids (1997) *Subversive Spirituality* Eerdmans
Reader, J. (1996) "Post-modernity and theological education" pps 12–21 in *British Journal
of Theological Education* vol 7 no. 3
Rogers, A. (1982) "Is theology an appropriate study for ordinands?" pps 354–358 in *Theology* LXXXV
Saint-Exupéry, A. de (1982) *The Little Prince* Piccolo/Pan
Savage, M. (1993) "Music, theology and Christian education" pps 16–22 in *British Journal
of Theological Education* vol 5 no. 3
Schick, G.V. (1960) *Luther's Works Volume 2. Lectures on Genesis* Concordia
Schofield, J. (1994) "It's not for me: or resisting theological reflection" pps 16–25 in *British
Journal of Theological Education* vol 6 no. 2
Schüssler-Fiorenza, F. (1996) "Thinking theologically about theological education" pps
318–341 in Astley, J., Francis, L.J. and Crowder, C. eds
Smith, G.T. (1996) "Spiritual formation in the academy. A unifying model" pps 83–91 in
Theological Education vol 33 no. 1
Stevens, W. (1965) *Selected Poems* Faber
Stone, H. and Duke, J.O. (1996) *How To Think Theologically* Fortress
Taylor, J.V. (1986) *A Matter of Life and Death* SCM (1992) *The Go-Between God. The Holy
Spirit and Christian Mission* SCM
Temple, W. (1940) *Nature, Man and God* Macmillan
Theological Institute (1992) *Provincial Curriculum* TISEC
Thomas, O.C. (1967) "Professional education and theological education" pps 556–563 in
Theological Education vol 4 no. 1 (1969) "Some issues in theological education" pps 346–356 in *Theological Education* vol 5
Thomas, R.S. (1993) *Collected Poems 1945–1990* Phoenix
Tracy, D. (1981) *The Analogical Imagination: Christian Theology and the Culture of Pluralism*
SCM
Troeger, T.H. (1990) *Imagining A Sermon* Abingdon
Vance, N. (1981) "Iris Murdoch's serious fun" pps 420–427 in *Theology* LXXXIV
Waal, E. de (1996) *A Seven Day Journey with Thomas Merton* Eagle
Warnock, M. (1976) *Imagination* Faber and Faber (1980) "Imagination – aesthetic and religious" pps 403–409 in *Theology* LXXXIII (1986) "Religious imagination" pps 142–157 in
Mackey, J.P. ed *Religious Imagination* Edin. Univ. Press (1989) "Imagination and knowledge" pps 363–365 in *Theology* vol XCII no. 749
Weil, S. (1959) *Waiting on God* Fontana/Collins
Welch, S.D. (1990) *A Feminist Ethic of Risk* Fortress Press
Westerhoff, J.H. (1982) "Theological education and models for ministry" pps 153–169 in
St Luke's Journal of Theology vol XXV no. 2
White, J.F. (1993) *Sacraments as God's Self Giving. Sacramental Practice and Faith* Abingdon
Williams, M. (1996) "Theological education and ordination training" pps 22–26 in *British
Journal of Theological Education* vol 8 no. 1
Williams, R. (1990) *The Wound of Knowledge* DLT
Wilson, P.S. (1988) *Imagination of the Heart. New Understandings in Preaching* Abingdon
(1995) *The Practice of Preaching* Abingdon

Wood, C.M. (1985) "Theological enquiry and theological education" pps 73–93 in *Theological Education* vol 21 (1996) "Theological education and education for church leadership" pps 303–314 in Astley, J., Francis, L.J. and Crowder, C. eds

Yates, W. (1992) "The future of the arts in theological education" pps 11–22 in *British Journal of Theological Education* vol 4 no. 3